T0083216

THE ANGEL
OF OBSESSION

Arkansas Poetry Award Series

THE ANGEL
OF OBSESSION

Poems by Julie Suk

THE UNIVERSITY OF ARKANSAS PRESS

FAYETTEVILLE   1992

Copyright 1992 by Julie Suk
All rights reserved
Manufactured in the United States of America
96 95 94 93 92   5 4 3 2 1

This book was designed by Chiquita Babb using the Bembo typeface.

The paper used in this publication meets the minimum requirements
of the American National Standard for Permanence of Paper for
Printed Library Materials z39.48-1984. ⊚

Library of Congress Cataloging-in-Publication Data

Suk, Julie.
      The angel of obsession / Julie Suk.
          p.   cm. — (Arkansas poetry award series)
      ISBN 1-55728-246-3 (alk. paper). — ISBN 1-55728-247-1
  (pbk. : alk. paper)
      I. Title. II. Series.
  PS3569.U255A84 1991
  811'.54—dc20   91-37208
                                                      CIP

iv

ACKNOWLEDGMENTS

Grateful acknowledgment is made to the editors of the following journals in which these poems first appeared: *Aura:* "Canada Geese"; *The Georgia Review:* "In the Garden of Earthly Delights"; *Kansas Quarterly:* "Falling to Sleep"; *Memphis State Review:* "Early and Late"; *Midwest Quarterly:* "Family"; *Negative Capability:* "Words I Won't Give Up On"; *New Letters:* "Smoldering"; *Plainsong:* "The Poem about Greece"; *Poetry:* "Beyond the Hill," "La Tempesta," "Playing against Sleep," "Quicksilver," "Remembering the Plot"; *The Poetry Review:* "Mortal Taste"; *River City:* "From the Stars, Silence," "Underworld"; *St. Andrews Review:* "Epitaph"; *Southern Humanities Review:* "A Cut in the Mountain," "In Eterno"; *Southern Poetry Review:* "The Path"; *Sou'wester:* "Floating Tethered," "Rain"; *Tar River Poetry:* "Chartres."

A number of these poems also appeared in *Heartwood*, Briarpatch Press, 1991. "Don't Tell Me," from the collection *North Carolina Poetry/The Eighties.* "Lost," and "Remembering the Plot," from the collection *Turning Dances.* "Mortal Taste," and "Waking the Stars," from the collection *Alabama Poets.* "Nothing to Do with Us," from the collection *Cardinal/Anthology of North Carolina Poets.*

CONTENTS

III

For Wythe and Palmer Whiting

I

"I feel odd talking to some little lights that keep going on and off without answering. At last after many nights it happened . . . a cascade of soft voices . . . colliding, intermingling. Very soon we could converse. And now they're my kinfolk."

Mario Vargas Llosa
The Storyteller

BEYOND THE HILL

*"It amuses me to imagine what is beyond a
hill. I want so much to represent those things I
will never see."*

Yves Tanguy

Above the spire across the street,
stars float like bell notes,
high, low, a clash of meteorites
scattering acids in space,
perhaps the people we've yet to meet,
not here but in another oasis.
Think how close we are.
I once found a fluted stone in a field.
The blade felt right to my hand
as if I had notched the sides
and thrown the shaft. But "why"
is a slippery dune hard to mount
without tumbling, the answer gritty.
If there were an ocean on the other side,
imagine sailing to a land
peopled with those we love and want back,
or—admit it—someone unknown,
the one we've looked for all our lives,
the one we'd sacrifice the others to meet.
The bank of clouds on the horizon,
now black, now gray, a silhouette
of hills and trees gradually filled
with the primaries—blood, bile,
the grief of blue,
and rushing to the foreground,
a commotion, a tease of randomness
that kinks the world we imagine
waving us into its arms.

IN THE GARDEN
OF EARTHLY DELIGHTS

Pale and unplucked, Eve kneels in the left panel,
her heart not yet driven to wander.
I envy the angels who fell around her.
In that dawn, tumbling naked and warm
to a mass of tattered wings,
did they tongue one another's wounds
and by that innocent act discover
how the body moves, how the hand
fingering plush skin divines
an underground river,
its caverns and whispers?

As animals begin to devour each other,
the sour taste of blood draws them back
again and again to lap from its pool.

It's the middle scene that excites us,
the carnal indifference,
the exotic sport of catch-as-catch-can.

But in the final panel the world comes true,
the sky exploding like a rotten fruit,
the landscape filled with the clatter of machines.
Cones of light lash over craters
where the wounded lie, skewered,
wings covered with ash,
their dreams rubble.

And there in the left foreground,
like children lost in a mob,
you and I face outwards, as if for rescue.
Urgent now, you lean on my breast and cling,
our tongues desperate from the heart's babel.

BIRTHDAY SONG

Maple buds break red to mingle
with the Judas trees now purpling.
The betrayer is my heart,
March taking its airs from rain
to soften towards April,
another year pulling me along.

But so much goes unrevealed,
tombs ransacked, names effaced.
When I climbed the final passageway
into Cheops' burial chamber, there,
high on the wall, was the name Belzoni,
nothing of who he was.

Also silent: hands outlined in caves,
hands we continue to clutch,
and let fall for other hands, hands
stroking as if that tracery would beget
its own gallery of echoes.

This morning I passed a sign:
SISTER LEISHA TELLS YOUR FUTURE
AND PAST. But I haven't the time.

It's Arbor Day, the day
they give away seedlings
of buckeye, peach, and river oak.
Time again for rooting blind,
the year's bitter pit,
succulent flesh.

IN ETERNO

"Memory, the ruins of experience."
Mark Stevens

Yes, I remember
the French clock on the mantel,
the boat on top
rocking the minutes away.
No, said my maiden aunt,
not even when she was young
did it run, maybe years before.

In eterno . . . in eterno . . .
Mahler ends his song,
and leaves us wondering
how much the earth sustains,
how much is tossed
or left unsung.
When my aunt died
I threw away the letters
hidden in a trunk.

"Dear Augusta, I'm sorry
it was to end like this,
causing such anguish,
but you were the one
who refused to leave
your father and the house.
Forgive me.
I will always . . ."

I burn more than I save,
but a dress in the attic
is dragging up dust,
a child talking to herself,
the dialogue between keys
and strings so resonant
we forget it's solo.
The words breathed in our ears,
"Tell how it was."

You wrote, ". . . your tears,
so beautiful . . .
I'll never forget . . ."
I had forgotten,
but not those shed an hour ago.
When I say I love you, believe
for a moment it's true.
We're born possessed
by a hunger to be born,
the closet emptied,
and crammed again,
books opened to lives,
the clock winding down
on the plot.

ORIGINAL SIN

After the act of love,
reason lies down, the past
and its angers covered,
moonlight mulling
over a mound of clothes,
the half-opened drawer
of a bedside table,
and the arabesque of limbs
sprawled in a tangle of sheets.

In a room across the hall,
the child covers his head and dares
not breathe too loud.

Later, when his father leaves
for good, the boy's shame
is for himself. He wonders
about that night, the bitter words
and whispers that followed,
what he could have reversed
to make his parents stay—
called out his fever perhaps,
and they would have come, hovering
with cool hands and warm murmurs,
no broken faith.

LA TEMPESTA

Like an ancient bend
reclaimed by the river,
the absence of fear
is filled with its own memory:

the time you were carried
trembling up steps to a landing
to wait out a storm,
your mother soothing you

with stories, her hold serene
as Giorgione's madonna
who nurses her child
against a raging background,

the muted façade of a town
flashed into life,
clouds thundering gray-green
across what seems no end

of a night torn by lightning.
Your mother's face illumined
as you lean to her warmth,
even then slight, and cooling

as the seconds shut down.
The stairwell, a darkness
you imagine pouring
through windows and doors

that won't close, your feet
mired as time thunders closer,
chasing you back into nightmares
that sometimes woke true.

You, the loss of all you've owned,
recover the memory of mother
and child as if coming home,
as if love lies

where you always pictured it,
in the calm of the storm.
Even when love lies,
it's the dream you cling to.

QUICKSILVER

I did what a child dares,
threw a thermometer on bathroom tile
to scatter mercury,
then with the tip of a finger
tapped the droplets into a kindred pool.

I see myself in each of my children.
Where are we headed, I want to know.
Not that I'm afraid of turns
or unmarked routes—
it's the going too fast.

Watch out, I caution
and step into space from library stairs,
a load of self-help books in my arms.
A man crosses the street to help me up.
We exchange names and numbers
before falling back to our ways,
odds and ends left jingling
in the pocket of the other's life.

Quicksilver, that sometime messenger,
sometime thief.

Rummaging through the attic,
my daughter and son find a violin
that belonged to my father.
I draw the bow across strings,

and we take turns pulling out sound,
notes flying off *spiritus mercurius*.
Talk scatters between us
until time to go.

Goodbye, they wave, and drive off,
the risk of mishap carried along.
Possibilities too—the alchemy of love
returning its vapors transformed:
a look, a voice, a touch,
glistening before me.

MORTAL TASTE

The year I traced over pictures
in *Paradise Lost* mother complained.
What she didn't read
was the body I craved
pitched headfirst and naked from heaven,
flesh, and its rabble of feathers,
an unquenchable fire.

Home from the hunt,
father dumped a rucksack of doves
on the kitchen table,
threw one still warm in my lap,
a dollop of blood
crusted on its breast.

I fled but soon crept back
to him sitting there,
legs spread,
guts and feathers spiraling down
to mound at his feet,
a tiny wafer of lung
lifted on the blade.
Doves simmered in a pan
splashed with peppered wine.

Wrapped in fragrance,
I feasted that night,
and since.

Now I never see birds
without thinking how shamed
they look stripped
but how sinfully good
they go down—like Eve,
her belly, when she left the garden,
lusciously plumped.

FAMILY

You listen for a rap on the door,
the sister and brother you never had,
the mother who died too soon,
the father who drifted away,
and you set the table to put them in place.
fork there, knife here—no,
wrong. You begin again,
rehearsing over and over
what you should have done, or will do.

But hope sends regrets,
and when the cat slinks back, growling,
fur frizzed by shadows flickering outside,
you think of your throw-away child
who came too soon,
closing your father's mouth,
your mother's eyes.

The ghost still kicks under your heart.
And when an owl lands on the roof
and blows away, wind shuffling the leaves,
everything and nothing is the same.
You drift room to room plumping pillows
and picking up.
A last shivering look into the night
as you draw the curtains.

One by one the rooms go out.
Dark trees lean toward the house.
Limbs scratch the window panes.
You whisper, "Come in."

LOVING TO DEATH

The children accuse me
of saying one thing meaning another.
I wake up complaining to the dark:
So what, if truth sleeps in twin beds,
that's no cause for divorce.

Falling back to sleep,
I make promises I know I'll break.
In the morning, familiar aromas
of shaving cream and toast,
the sun pooled in a cup of tea.
News on television flashes
from scene to scene—arms laid down;
in a square, thousands of jubilant shouts,
the air so cold breath hovers
like a cartoon balloon
filled with simple words,
no double-talk.

Only the old, bundled in memory, weep
and wait for more tanks to come
rumbling from a cornered street
toward a soft sprawl of bodies,
the sons and daughters we love to death.

I turn savage with my children.
"Wake up," I demand,
"you've slept long enough."

And I make New Year promises,
a few I'm sure to keep:
I will die,
I will take my memories with me,
and leave survivors tossing in theirs.

WORDS I WON'T GIVE UP ON

For my father

Toward the end,
rarely more than whispers,
the tumor on your brain
packed around words
that wander in and out.

The room dimmed by blinds
and a brick wall,
my aimless chatter
tumbling around you
like a child who won't sit still.

You, my father,
staring over me
at a bawling soap opera
as I lift your hand,
clean the nails,
push back cuticles
to reveal bruised half-moons
I know say
what I can't speak of.

Too late,
nurse comes with the medicine
we encourage you to drink.

Look at me.

Pulling back your hand,
you wave at needling shadows
flicked across TV,
the words I want to say
static in my mouth.

FALLING TO SLEEP

Some of us go to bed scared,
Einstein for one, afraid
if he slept he would fall through.

Perhaps he forgot how the girl in the fairy tale
fell down the well of her dream
into the arms of a prince
who held her ever after
from milking cows.

Maybe he thought of the man
who walked in his sleep, yelled
                              "Thief!"
and shot his wife.

Dreams confuse, have energy without mass,
a jumbled equation scrawled on a blackboard
erased at sunrise.

A friend calls, threatening her life.
Her nightmare is the mouth emptied of words.

What I fear most is seeing the night through.
Not the dream, but its grotesque tatter
flapping at day.

I once saw a man force his child
to the window of a wrecked car,

hold the boy's head over the dead
and shout, "Look! Look!"

I change beds, roam the house, read
the mind is charted into hemispheres,
some oriented left, others right.

The day is touch as touch can,
but the dream is a reflection on multiple mirrors,
no end to the depth.
It is the scent haunting a forgotten room,
a door that opens on the dead,
the countless unborn,
and the few we ever really knew.
It is the love we live for a time,
and the hate, guiltless, true.

SMOLDERING

Propped up in his coffin,
my grandfather looked like the mummy of Seti I.

When my turn comes,
I want to die holding what I love,
the way windows catch as buildings rise
in a flare of sun.

Sometimes I wake trussed in my own arms,
the heart pressed down in its chest, smoldering.
Then I move to you, fumbling the body
as if there were treasure hidden in its shroud,
as if it were possible to sink beyond pain,
and surface forgetful of where we had been.

Morning, and the street rumbles through a day
like any other. Earth is peopling again,
and we unfold, thirsty as lotus seeds
lifted from a tomb.

II

"... people who live in the imaginary eyes of those who are not present. They are the dreamers."

Milan Kundera
The Unbearable Lightness of Being

WAKING THE STARS

"I have a new study of a starry night."
Vincent van Gogh

The village moon-soaked;
church and spire hunched
like an animal with one ear cocked,
the seething sky crashing blue-black
over stars.

I once fell asleep on a beach
and woke in a fall of such stars,
fragments of a dream drifting off,
the moon shrouded as this one is,
only not the improbable
orange-yellow-green.
None of this is real, not the town
or its turquoise froth of trees
lapping at blackened roofs,
nor the ecstatic cypress raking the sky.

The beach, a blanket embedded with grit,
the body lying next to me,
and the name I've forgotten,
they were real, not these fierce stars
staring like beasts at a fire,
nor the sleepers
wrapped in dreams we can't share.

If any one of those villagers
opened a window to look out,
he would drown in that sky:

a flake of plankton
feeding a night that never fills.
It is madness to run through the streets
pounding doors,
waking the dreams locked inside.

NOTHING TO DO WITH US

An owl hoots from a nearby tree.
A siren floats off down the street.
Lying here covered by the warm night,
I don't want to think of torn flesh.

Once while we slept,
your fingers dug into my thigh.
I was bruised for days.

So tender are we to touch,
the body reacts without knowledge,
not because of it,
mumbling along even as we die,
the way an animal brought down
continues to kick
while a spasm of guts spirals out.

Don't tell me that old wives' tale
about the owl call, not now,
the moon resting like a benediction
on the bed where we sprawl
exhausted by love.

ANGELS THAT KEEP US

In the darkness a mist hovers close
and you wake damp with longing.

It's the angel of dreams,
the one who leaves you undone,
a scent of sex in the air,
the feckless shadows fading.

All you remember is a delicious tongue
probing your ear.

That's why the angel of no-nonsense
demands day. He's the one
who stares into your eyes
during moments so intimate or cruel
you look the other way.

Isn't this what you wanted?
Honesty? Undivided attention?

When night comes back to roost,
insomnia swoops down hard,
pinions raking your flesh.

For hours you're captive
to a persistent harangue
like a willful child
banging a piano,

the angel of obsession
dragging a wing on the ground.
And you follow,
indifferent to those left
calling your name.

SLEEPERS

We graze on the edge of sleep,
far off the lowing of a train.
You pull me closer as if I might leave,
the train lulling us into a kind of slumber
to dream where we've been, or want to be.

Once when we came to a stop,
I lifted the shade to my berth
and a man from another life stared back
waiting to take your place.

Sleek and oiled, trains slide over bare lands,
stations where Indians hold up beads,
their faces an empty plain.
And I'm the child on the bike,
waving at arrivals I dream will be mine.
Gone. The dead, the dying—
all those who leave—sleepers
rattling back and forth.

Miles slow when we look into the distance
where mountains anchor the memories
of oceans and ancient fires.
And the past we'd like to excavate,
playing the story over, this time on cue,
filling in people we missed:
a terminus we might never reach,
the train pouring out of our lives.

DREAMING THE DEAD

"All who leave the earth go to the moon which
is swollen by their breath during the first half of
the month."

From the Upanishads

That's when the moon gives us hell,
dogs in the neighborhood crouched in a howl,
and the dead all talking at once.
You'd think there were better things to do
than loll around in dreams,
but the dead don't mind, they can't wait
to be called into beds where we sprawl
with our gowns hiked up, can't wait
to dump their grievances.
And when we close in with excuses,
they give us the brush-off.
Writing down what was done or said
won't recover the plot as it was.
Fitful faces dissolve and remake,
luring us again through scene after scene,
the moon tugging, desire waxing.
Tonight I wished on a shooting star,
but the kettle whistles for tea,
and the cry of a wakeful child
demands a story that turns on light.
These are our saviors
when the moon spins us foolish.
I think of the wishes I made
and how lucky I am so few came home.

CANADA GEESE

I hear them before they come into sight
clipping a swath of mist
as they move diagonally across
sweet-gum and oak, the call
poignant as a night train
approaching half-sleep,
the dream it interrupts, here and gone,
fading into the dark.
A kind of bruise we find on the body,
not remembering what brought it about.

REMEMBERING THE PLOT

Today drifts into yesterday.
Difficult to remember
the food eaten, rooms cleaned.

Same with books. You read,
read, but recall only
that someone floated off,

finally, from years of solitude,
and danced naked in a bowler hat.
But the nose has a better memory,

whole lives waft back, the moments
that linger in limbo
pulled out by a random scent.

And you stand in the street
watching a cab drive off
leaving in its wake

the aroma of a man's cigarette
that even now revives
the way his fingers pressed

deep into your thigh,
the hairs on his wrist
suddenly stricken with sunlight.

DON'T TELL ME

Don't tell me the dream I've heard
time and again,
the nightmare that fails to catch you
flying, luckily, above it all,
your body jerked up before it lands
sound awake in bed,
the mound a pillow not a grave,
teeth, bones, flesh intact,
the warm breath sleeping next to you
the one constant.
Don't tell me.
For every dream like that,
another splatters rock-bottom,
refusing to evaporate.
Don't tell me how we run
slow-motion to escape,
the ground an escalator
winding the opposite way, or, worse,
the road we arrive on
going as we come.
Don't tell me the people we meet
flip from face to face.
I believe what I dream.
When the train on the other rail
slides back and leaves
an illusion of moving forward,
I ride that.
Don't tell me the face at the window
is only reflection,

a life conjured
the moment it flashes by.
Don't tell me it was my mouth
pressed against glass.
Don't tell me the mouth is a dream.

HOW WE MOVE AWAY

He fills the bird feeder,
and looks out over the treeline.
Nothing seems the same.
Two stages of pine have dropped into hardwoods,
the once deep and pungent
now a constriction circling the heart.

She walks up behind him
and wraps her arms around his waist,
breasts pressed against his wings.
He likes that feel of a Sunday afternoon
but not his mood rearranged.
"I'm going for a walk," he says,
"a walk," and closes the gate.
Once out, he opens his fist,
his wife's sing-song fading.

He knows he'll soon turn and go home,
take the woman in his arms
and murmur consolations in her ear.
And there are shrubs to trim,
the patio to clean, whatever flew
so far out of himself now caged,
only this turbulence beating inside,
fed by the salt and lime of his life.

NOT LOST

No cryptograph on the car ahead.
The stark red on white
license plate reads
I AM LOST
I want to drive alongside
and shout, *Wait!*
there's a map
for the state you're in.
But that's a lie.
Despite caution signs
I drift to the wrong lane,
absorbed in a couple
on the sidewalk
who waver toward one another
but never quite meet,
she desperate, he distant,
as they turn a corner
and out of sight.
Once I rode a bus for hours
through the city,
people on, off
with the story of their lives,
strays I may never again see.
And you, and you,
who fell through my love,
are still out of touch
but I won't say lost,
a shadow away
lengthening behind me.

RAIN

The sound of rain purls around us—
curve, hollow, all the retreats we fish in—
the world a far-off thunder in the mountain,
not twisted bodies swept down-canyon.

We float off to sleep in a tangle of limbs,
the bed an ark filled with our beasts,
the dream more than once flying out
in search of a landing place.

Rain rails against the window
as if its life depended on us to open up.
The words *I love you* pour, and then drought
until the next deluge greens.

Before water runs bitter,
there is a place back in the hills,
a stream so clear you would hope a hunter,
dropping to rest, would look at his bloody hands
and decide *no, not here*.

Here, we lie like any two rivers
that come together, casualties piled in our wake.
We soothe one another for a time and forgive
how easily the unwanted are drowned.

Even as it pummels the land,
rain softens the dead.
Muttering in retreat, it smears a stain
across the ceiling above our bed.
Even now you drift away.

FROM THE STARS, SILENCE

Listen one says but the other doesn't

The usual
Shouting over a great distance
Static the answer

Or the long silence of a bottle
Bobbing on the ocean

If it were possible
To gather all the wasted words
Which would I keep
Which would keep you

I bump into the warm stall of your body
Yes I love you yesyes

Words can take or leave gravity
I like to think they graze between stars

Mine, yours
In a dumb way close
Until a tongue calls them home

AFTER IT'S OVER
AND YOU'RE THE LAST ONE

What will you do
once you stack the wood by the door,
spread potatoes and apples
in the cellar, collect traps, guns,
matches, seed and hoe?

Snow falls for days,
and days fall too in a smothering pile.
All you know is that light comes, goes,
with the same drifts of silence,
no tracks to follow except your own,
at night your gown pulled tight
in your crotch while you dream
someone else on the pillow.

The morning continues barren,
a white sheet you scribble,
no assurance the one you write for
will come. You wait for a catch
of breath, a knock on the door.

And maybe he enters,
stomping his boots on the mat,
steam rising from his coat,
his look soft as drift
when you raise your eyes, touch,
explore, pelt against pelt,
cries falling from your mouths as one,
the rime on your thighs not ice.

After it's over,
you reach for succor, sympathy, and love,
but not long.
A hunger you can't lay down
forces you to leave.
More alone than ever, what will you do
if silence refuses to melt into words?

EARLY AND LATE

The first bird chips into dawn
as if all the sounds ever made
had hardened there.

Even now someone is crying
and we won't hear.

I turn to your side of the bed,
but you wander off in a dream,
that haven where the body can let go
and not care if we fall,
disaster flicked off so slightly
you might think it an eyelash,
the dream blinking on despite the loss.

It's the morning we suffer,
in and out of arms.
Now they lay us down, here,
where dreams are grounded in blood.
So sleep . . .
there is still time
before the one last star
explodes into day,
time before the nightmare cry
comes aloud.

Half awake, I stand on the doorstep,
ink on the morning paper still damp,
my hands smearing the words.

III

"By now the battle is joined between those that exist and would like to be eternal and us who don't exist and would like to . . ."

Italo Calvino
t zero

FALLEN UNTO TEARS

From a painting by Antonello da Messina

Hers isn't the usual
cherubic face.
This angel looks used,
as if she's been around
long enough to call
sorrow her home,
as if, street-wise,
nothing up to now
could ruffle her.

Wings tell the story,
the plumage buzzard-black,
a streak of crimson
on the folds.

The crucified body,
propped against her shoulder,
is strung with clotted blood
from a gash under his breast,
mouth slack, eyes slit
to indifference.

As she leans forward
to catch the backward thrust,
one arm twines around his,
her face turned so
that we get the full impact
of those unexpected tears.

The ground around them
is strewn with grave-spill,
skulls, bones, without name.
In the far distance,
a few figures mill
around a cross.

The angel's sorrow is utter.
She seems to know something
we don't, but the body
is too heavy for her to lift.
Even if she could,
where would they go?

LA DOLCE VITA

The woman steps down from the bus
into a swarm of paparazzi,
a new dress under her arm,
not a cloud smearing the sky.
She has yet to learn
her children and husband are dead.
Murder. Suicide.

Story after story, the same
sun-bathed day,
muted guns at the border,
women berry-picking in a field near town.
I gave my love a willow sprig they sing.
A few kilometers away, the enemy
slips through the forest.

Say happiness is suspect,
reason enough to knock on wood
before the axe swings.
Barbed questions catch us
trying to escape.
Were the women left sprawled
across rows of blood?
Were the children asleep
when the father raised his gun?

Say we're incapable of certain acts.
Say it again.

Boxcars rattle through the countryside,
crammed with the fear
that this is not just a change of camps.
The pitch night swells with screams,
the ground between trees
strewn with owl pellets,
those indigestible remains
of lives swallowed whole.

PLAYING AGAINST SLEEP

There are nights I fight sleep,
dizzy sometimes with success,
my dreams left lusting for more.

Don't get me wrong,
I love the easy seductions,
the costumes and masks,
the garbled lines,
one person merging into another.

But the play moves on,
scrambling scenes in the dark,
no one answering to cues.

Same as those faces
we see on the evening news,
children dying in roles
they haven't rehearsed.

"Mama, they're killing me!"
Rufina Amaya hears her son scream—
somewhere in the carnage
a husband sprawled dead.

And there the dialogue ends,
but the cries follow us,
follow all day and into our sleep,
assuming the nightmare.

Too much for this woman
on the front row.
Not even an "Excuse me"
when she crashes out.

A CUT IN THE MOUNTAIN

Fast as we build roads
between the cities of want and have,
monsters fall out of rock—
tracks, trails, bones, teeth,
impressions on shale
jumbled as a picture puzzle.

Not knowing what to expect,
we collect rocks and fossils,
tame them on tables and shelves,
stack them in gardens,
border the beds.

Examining the fine print of dendrites,
which look like fossils but aren't,
I think how figments gull us to belief,
while the real brute waits
to break out of shadow.

And what of the first, delicate
small-frame bones—
who would have expected
the later *tyrannos*?

If you were to find me limed in stone,
vestiges of beads, smudge that was silk,
outlining my skeleton,
would you wonder about the axe in my hand?

EXECUTIONS, MAY 1814

When asked why he painted such scenes, Goya
replied, "To have the pleasure of saying eternally
to men that they should stop being barbarians."

At first I couldn't understand
why the soldiers had been described
in such a bad light
 some so young
  sweet-faced as my own son

A day like any other
flips into night and madness.
The dead sprawl on the dead,
others huddle against the wall,
waiting to be executed.
One man gnaws his knuckles
as if drawing the last
succor from flesh.
Desperate for disbelief,
another covers his face.
The priest kneels with folded hands,
though at this point
prayer is hysterical rote.

Our children float through the streets
like shadows. The sick, the dying,
soon to follow the dead
we no longer have the strength to bury.

All the redolent droppings—
religion, art, reason, love—
splat into fear.

But the central figure,
focused in lantern light,
chooses heroics.
Rapt with despair,
he flings his arms wide
defying his assassins.

Round and round tethered to this question:
What more can they lose by trying to escape?

The men in the death squad stand
in a row of blurred profiles
as if they were privy
to right and wrong,
victims too of bloodshed.

This for my poor dead wife.
This for my son. My son!
I dream, but you can't call it sleep.

Guns extended, each rifleman
prepares to shoot and move on,
perhaps to the town over the hill.

I watched my mother   they held me
took her   all of them
the baby's skull   crushed flowers
they took her   she running
running into the burning house.

Again the fixed bayonets,
the repetitive clickclick,
the heart's burst, a red flare.

There is no place to turn from the dead,
the unbearable silence.
Silence, the ultimate abuse we inflict.
At least from screams we know there is life.

UNDERWORLD

*Twenty-foot python found living under house
in Orlando.*

He thought the racket that morning
was from cats, until he looked
out in time to see
a coon swallowed headfirst,
feet kicking to the last.

The snake must have crawled
the neighborhood at night to feed.
You'd think someone driving home late
would have seen it sliding
across the road.

Maybe lovers parked under the oak
could sense how close danger looped,
a breath caressing the neck,
a stroke down the back.

"Lock your doors!"
every mother cries,
knowing how love
can squeeze us to death.

Thought of that crawl space
chills—the cold, fixed eyes,
the heat-seeking mouth,
the hiss of the furnace as it blows
the darkness into our lives.

The horror grows,
a trail of regurgitated bones,
children, maybe, who wandered
and never came home.

Housed in our underworld,
a cold menace feeds
on nightmares. Any day
we'll be found out.

REHEARSING DEATH

I

El Salvador, 1978

The day ends like this:
he slams the bolt on their screams,
washes gore from his hands,
and orders his driver
to help with his boots. At home,
his wife meets him in the foyer.
He slides one hand up and down her back,
the other massages her breasts.
They go upstairs.
You could say he's efficient.

II

Hamburg, 1934

Hours go by,
the day is dark as night.
We lie on our backs
as if buried alive,
listening to the sound of boots
as the men search the house.
The floor overhead shakes.
I imagine him lifting the boards,
a smile on his face as he kneels

to stroke my cheek
with the barrel of his gun.
Open your mouth, he commands.

III

Argentina, 1977

Pain is an echo
that screams back
again, again.
In time I'm numbed
by the unspeakable things they do—
nine men—but I tell nothing,
have nothing to tell, except
that you and I are friends—
you, my once-lover. Love
a word I no longer know,
its exquisite tortures aborted.

IV

Warsaw, 1944

Some things we escape,
but it's impossible
to rub from sight
the truckloads—men, women,

children—lined up and shot
ka puck ka puck,
then kicked in a ditch,
their eyes gouged out.
Is it because the dead
have a dark way of staring into us
I still hear the cries?

V

Is it because we are taught
turn the one cheek,
then the other,
it could be an angel you meet
that we are willing to plead,
yes, yes there is reprieve,
only at the last
slipping our arms
into death's frayed sleeves?

CHARTRES

I could be anywhere in the States.
The train, a local, kids in jeans,
scrubby towns strung between stations.
Only the red-tiled roofs
and confusion of language seem out of place.
Then Chartres, perched on its hill,
wings pressed against walls
that hold other walls from tumbling,
the town sprawled at the base.

And I'm on my knees at the sight.
The mutation of stone into glass—
sapphire, rose, chrysoprase—
a kaleidoscope of slivers
held in the middle of a turn.

To think that a manic order
could bring it to ruin.

The poor still give alms
and the sick are no better,
but the saints look humanly down
as if, at this moment,
they had stepped to the porch for air.
No matter that they crumble.
The lamp is on the nail.
Nothing much changed,
only the more impossible ways we die,
not these stones, the rapture,
rising for now out of our hands.

THE BEAUTIFUL LIES OUTSIDE

For Ellie

In this picture of us as children
I hold your hand, all smiles.
You hang back scowling
at the year that pulls us into focus.
In the background a path wavers house to house
through a field no longer there.

Today when I call your hospital room
I look for a way to lift.
It's solace you want. And we've never lied.
"What a lovely day," I try.

I remind you of those summer nights
your father lifted us onto his shoulders
to name the stars as if naming
would hold them on course.
They still glide through watch after watch,
darkness slipping in to sabotage.

I want the sun to break across the horizon
and wash us gold, but my driveway
is stained by mist, a fine rain
that falls unseen unless I stand outside
and feel its ghost,

the gentle touch and go
barely registered by trees
lost in their deep indifferent green.
Before it pours, I promise to pull in
all the beautiful lies.

EPITAPH

I don't want the chiseled slab,
its name and date fading into gray,
I want the angel in the old cemetery,
the classy one whose wings are fluffed,
and right leg flexed
as if about to take off,
the one who all these years
tried to whisper in my ear as I ran by
with plastic flowers in my arms.

I want to lie down stripped
under its weight,
my hands no longer fists,
its breath grazing my flesh—

me, the one who falls into my life
thinking, sure, I can fix up the place.
But bones expose themselves
despite perpetual care,
and the mole gouges,
snout and claws finding me out.

I want to rise,
hanging on for dear, dear life,
the way I rode shoulders
when I was a child, want to step out
into a jungle of temples lost in people
we're bound to stumble across,

my angel and I singing together
in a crazy off-day way,

my angel with chipped nose,
and bird shit on its wings.

THE PATH

For Guy Owen

The path isn't responsible.
Wandering off, it sometimes splits,
or ends at briar patch and field,
like the trail I took today
following the mountain foot.

Did the first ones to find this place
stand and stare
across blue-eyed grass and berry bush,
the path broken, abandoned
to thin lines running off at random
like pottery craze?

What is it about this clearing
that scatters us?
Each lost in the self,
swallowed by the dark implosion of leaves,
or drawn to the glitter of mica,
galaxy after galaxy
embedded in the cold range,
out of reach until stone crumbles
and light drifts.

I put my foot in your step,
and our bodies pick up the same dust.
Rising, settling to rise again,
it is a permanence impossible to shake
once we enter its universe.

THE POEM ABOUT GREECE

The poem about Greece refuses to end.
It runs on like a water color, blending
the way sky and sea touch and let go,

from time to time flooding our lives
as if the gods still spoke
and we understood.

Diving in, we bring up fragments.
A hand matches an arm, stones engage,
the vase holds.

In the temple, a crazy old woman
babbles for translation.

Again we're thrown into a sea
that holds us buoyant
so long as we breathe,

a panic of fish scattering,
blue-green turning up bronze and gold.

FLOATING TETHERED

*"My stay here goes forward, which is not to say
I am anywhere near finishing."*

Claude Monet

I

Days drift by,
and the further away we stand,
the clearer they reflect.
Layer over layer of flowers, trees, shrubs,
mirrored on water, wisteria so purple-plumped
it spills, and colors continue to pour,
what can't be seen
moving under the surface.

Grass sways at the bottom of a pond,
a quiver of stalks splays into lilies,
lilies floating tethered,
the way a long-submerged memory
floats up,
    surprised
by a furious shower of light.

II

Light travels through space like an ice-crack,
splintering when it hits.
We swim into color, flushed,
someone there to stroke us into shape.

When the wobbling head of my son
broke those waters,
the wet warm smack of his mouth
startled runnels of milk down my breast.

The heart pumps out, and I forget
how the tide leaves us strewn,
rock crumbled, the planet shunting its crust.

III

To slow our drop into darkness,
I sleep holding on to you.

And dig into the body as if it held a gem
that would keep the rest of our lives
unflawed, dig until the voice cries out in a tongue
we all speak but rarely understand.

Maybe one day we'll strike a vein
filled with crystals,
and find ourselves waiting to be born
red, gold, black,
and for once transparent,
held in a flash-fire
face to face with love.

IV

Racing away with our memories,
the galaxies recede in all directions.
The older I become,
the further back I reflect
on those I first held close.

Out there in the milky way of childhood,
I ride on my father's shoulders
to watch a parade, the night torch-lit,
figures flickering by in costumes and masks.

You lie nearer and warm,
but what do I really know of you,
or myself? When you hold me, I'm lost,
the body darting off like a child.

V

A million years ago,
fire slumbered among hammer stones,
chips, pieces of bone.

A woman runs and falls by the shores of a lake,
gets up, falls again to stay
covered by volcanic ash, the body emptied,
only an outline left to recall.

But the dead continue to root:
a profusion of graves,
the raped and shot covered with leaves,
the shattered brushed over.

Upstairs in dreams,
we ignore the creaking floors.
A log shifts
and a shower of sparks hits the hearth.
You murmur, turn, and we fall back to sleep,
the rug left smoldering.

VI

Nightmares sometimes repeat,
but with variations
so that we can say
    It won't be like this next time
next time we move in, again
on the same faultline.

VII

The moon bobs free
from a stroke of cloud,
one side plucked off,
the next night smaller,
and smaller,
until only a petal remains,

but enough
that we continue to believe
in the body making its slow way back,
whole again.

VIII

You surface in every face,
so close I feel the life lived before,
a wilderness cluttered with remains,
the planet wasting us age to age,
the body changing like weather on radar.

When you come,
the hairs on my thighs rise
like grass after rain.

Once more to taste your tongue,
the words you leave in my mouth.

And after the sweet sloughing of flesh,
and gradual descent through fault and stress,
the bones of memory click in place
to reconstruct what we lost—
a revenant come home.
I have loved you all my lives.

Author of three chapbooks, Julie Suk is the associate editor of *Southern Poetry Review* and lives in Charlotte, North Carolina.